THEN *&* NOW

MARYLAND
WORKBOATS

MARYLAND WORKBOATS

Byshe Hicks

To Mom Mom (Betty Flottemesch), who passed away while I was writing this book—a fellow historian with whom I enjoyed long talks about the old days.

Library of Congress Control Number: 2009921033

Published by Arcadia Publishing
Charleston, South Carolina

Printed in the United States of America

Then and Now is a registered trademark and is used under license from
Salamander Books Limited

For all general information contact Arcadia Publishing at:
Telephone 843-853-2070
Fax 843-853-0044
E-mail sales@arcadiapublishing.com
For customer service and orders:
Toll-Free 1-888-313-2665

Visit us on the Internet at www.arcadiapublishing.com

ON THE FRONT COVER: The bugeye *Edna E. Lockwood* was built on Tilghman Island in 1889 and is one of the last of her kind left. Bugeyes were developed around the 1860s to dredge oysters. They are direct descendants of the log canoes. The hull of the bugeye is comprised of several dug-out logs fastened together. The name is derived from the hawes pipes on the bow, which are said to look like eyes. (Now courtesy of the author; then courtesy of the Chesapeake Bay Maritime Museum.)

ON THE BACK COVER: This buy boat would typically be used to buy oysters off the skipjacks, which would save them from having to discharge in port. In this case, though, they have put dredges on her to gather seed oysters. The State of Maryland grows seed, or juvenile, oysters in designated areas to later be dredged up and transplanted to depleted beds. Oystermen are paid for this, as it benefits both the oyster population and the watermen. (Photograph by Robert de Gast, courtesy of the Chesapeake Bay Maritime Museum.)

Contents

Acknowledgments   vii
Bibliography   viii
Introduction   ix

1.   Oystering   11

2.   Crabbing and Other Fisheries   27

3.   Workboat Harbors   37

4.   Cargo   53

5.   Passengers   65

6.   Boatyards   75

7.   Where Are They Now?   83

ACKNOWLEDGMENTS

I came across many generous people while writing this book, and without them, none of it would have happened. Back when I worked on the skipjack *Martha Lewis*, the Chesapeake Bay Maritime Museum—CBMM—in St. Michael's was always a great help. The guys in the shop would always stop what they were doing and show me how to caulk a seam or serve a rope, for instance. While writing this book, their library staff was just as helpful, particularly curator Pete Lesher. The same goes for the staff of the Calvert Marine Museum in Solomon's Island. Both museums do an excellent job of preserving the culture and perpetuating the history of the bay. As long as they are around, none of this history will disappear.

There have also been many people I have come across who were a great help. Katie Duncan with Vane Brothers was a big help in letting me research their library, as was Jerry Smith at the Smith Shipyard, with whom I enjoyed talking about the old yard. Many of their tidbits of knowledge have contributed to this book.

I cannot forget my fellow crewmembers on the tugboat *Harriet Moran*. They have been very accommodating while working on this book. I am sure they will be glad to know that it's finally finished.

Last, but far from least, is my wife, Becky, who has been a great help with this book. We met when she volunteered on the *Martha Lewis*, and we both have a great fondness for that boat. She is now the coauthor on the book of our lives together. Unless indicated, all photographs are from the author's collection.

BIBLIOGRAPHY

Brewington, M. V. *Chesapeake Bay: A Pictorial Maritime History*. Cambridge, MD: Cornell Maritime Press, 1953.

Burgess, Robert H. *Chesapeake Circle*. Cambridge, MD: Cornell Maritime Press, 1965.

———. *Chesapeake Sailing Craft*. Cambridge, MD: Tidewater Publishers, 1975.

———. *This Was Chesapeake Bay*. Cambridge, MD: Cornell Maritime Press, 1963.

Davies, Mary Butler. *Time and the Tide: A Centennial History of the Vane Brothers Company*. Vane Brothers Company, 1998.

Keith, Robert C. *Baltimore Harbor: A Picture History*. Baltimore, MD: Ocean World Publishing Company, 1982.

Vojtech, Pat. *Chesapeake Bay Skipjacks*. Centreville, MD: Tidewater Publishers, 1993.

INTRODUCTION

When the first Europeans came to the Chesapeake Bay, what they found were an indigenous people with watercraft well suited to their needs. They built dugout canoes out of the plentiful, large trees.

On the other hand, Europeans used a plank on frame construction. When these two cultures met, the results were boats being built using both methods. Seemingly European-looking boats would have hulls built of one or more dugout logs. This was the beginning of a unique style of craft distinctive to Chesapeake waters.

Working boats are designed to do the intended job in the particular waters they work. Their design is dictated by practicality. Variables include water depth, number of sustainable crew, ergonomics, size of cargo, and prevailing winds, to name just a few. This is why boats can be recognized from their region.

The Chesapeake Bay is a shallow, protected estuary with relatively light winds. This is why bay boats are often characterized by a low freeboard and large sail area. Knowing this, one could look at any boat in the world and get a general idea of the type of work and type of water in which she works.

Building materials and ease of construction are also major factors in the design of a boat. Early on in Maryland's history, many boats were built of whole trees dug or hewn out. These trees later became scarcer and were replaced with smaller planks. The bugeye is a good example of that. This boat evolved from the dugout canoe and was constructed of several logs drifted together. As this resource dwindled, builders used plank on frame construction while retaining the same hull shape.

As the resource of the oyster harvest dwindled, a whole new boat replaced the outdated bugeye. The skipjack evolved from the simple flat-bottomed boats of Long Island Sound. Hampton flatties were brought down to take advantage of the bay's more than bountiful oyster population. As the harvest was being overfished, these simple boats morphed into the larger skipjack in the late 1800s and replaced the bugeye.

Skipjacks were cheap and easy to build. Their construction is of the deadrise type. This is a flat bottom with a shallow V shape. The planks are short, flat, and set at a roughly 90-degree angle to the keel. It makes for quick and easy building or maintenance. The construction is crude and simple, but the boat still retains a graceful, aesthetic appearance. Early on, some referred to the skipjacks as "deadrise boats," but what we call a deadrise today is the small powered vessel that has come to dominate our workboat harbors. The hull is of the same basic cross plank construction. They are much like the pickup trucks of the bay, even in appearance, with the cabin forward and the open working area aft. These boats can be interchanged with various fishing gear throughout the season. One can oyster, crab, clam, or even work as a head boat taking out anglers for rockfish.

Working harbors have seen much change throughout the years. Waterman towns such as Rock Hall or Oxford, once with a majority of workboats, are now dominated by yachts and new development. When at one time boatyards could bend and fasten a 2-inch plank, they now specialize in fiberglass repair. What was once a hardware store that sold oilskins and galvanized fastenings now is a national chain yachting store selling signal flag belts and leather boat moccasins. Condominiums are squeezing into almost any available waterfront property. Unsustainable development and culture are duking it out in a fight to the death.

Baltimore is also going through a lot of these changes, but it is still very much a working harbor. The reason for being such a busy port is the proximity to the Midwest. Baltimore Harbor is the closest eastern seaport to the Midwest. Cargo can be shipped to and from Baltimore and then put on rail or truck for a shorter overland route.

When boats transit to or from the North, they will often take the Chesapeake and Delaware Canal. The C&D Canal opened in 1829, connecting Broad Creek in Maryland and St. Georges Creek in Delaware. Schooners called rams were designed to transit this narrow passage. These slab-sided, flat-bottomed boats worked well to maximize the amount of cargo through minimal width and depth of water. They also eliminated the use of top masts in order to fit under the bridges.

Smaller bay craft such as schooners, bugeyes, and skipjacks connected the towns of the bay. These vessels brought produce, lumber, and passengers to the bigger cities like Baltimore and then brought back goods such as coal, cans, sugar, and oil.

In 1813, the first steamboat on the bay, named *Chesapeake*, was put into service under the Union Line. There soon followed many more vessels like this that connected towns with cities. They soon became the quick and more reliable transportation of choice on the bay. The steamers worked until the early 1960s carrying goods and people. They were not able to survive the advent of trucks, buses, and highways.

The boats working Maryland water today are a mix of traditional bay craft and modern steel boats, like tugs and barges. Fewer of the boats are indigenous to these waters. On the bright side, there are many people up and down the bay keeping up traditions and preserving these boats. Whether they are the new generation of apprentices at the CBMM or watermen scraping out a living on the bay, they are all holding an important part of this country's culture.

CHAPTER 1

OYSTERING

One of the oldest and, at one time, most profitable methods of fishing in Maryland, oystering dates back to the Native Americans with dugout canoes. Since European settlement, several methods and boats have evolved to harvest the bivalve, and some are still being used today. The boats pictured above are two-masted schooners off-loading in Baltimore. (Courtesy of the Library of Congress.)

The Chesapeake log canoe is the result of two very different cultures coming together in the 16th and 17th centuries. When the Europeans came to the Chesapeake, they adopted and embellished upon the native dugout canoe. Log canoes are no longer worked but are very actively raced. Regattas in St. Michael's and Oxford are held annually. These specialized vessels are recognized by their extreme sail area and crew hiking out on boards placed to windward. (Now photograph by A. Aubrey Bodine, © Jennifer Bodine, courtesy of www.AAubreyBodine.com; Then courtesy of the Library of Congress.)

This man is tonging from his log canoe. He will place what he scoops up with the tongs onto the culling board. Then he will sort through this catch, tossing the keepers to the side. The culling board is then tilted up, and the contents are dumped overboard. This is repeated either all day or until he catches his limit. Not much has changed for the tongers, but the oysters are much less plentiful. (Courtesy of the Library of Congress.)

These log canoes are rafted up to what looks like a two-masted schooner. The schooner is a market boat buying the oysters from the tongers. The market boats anchored near the oyster beds and saved the tongers time from having to go into port to off-load. Many of these schooners were later converted to power vessels called buy boats. These vessels are easily recognized by the wheelhouse set far aft and the topping lift used to lift the oysters. (Courtesy of the Library of Congress.)

These gentlemen are using a hand winder, although it is most likely a staged photograph, considering their dress. Winding dredges up by hand about every 5 to 10 minutes was a backbreaking job. Unsuspecting immigrants and drunken men were often shanghaied to do this laborious task. The gasoline engine was later used, making it an easier though noisier job. With the engine running, a crew member just had to pull the lever that engaged the clutch to haul in the dredge. The captain had a string that was attached to the throttle. He could stay at the helm and pull the string in order to let the crew know when to haul and to bring the dredges in quickly. (Both courtesy of the Library of Congress.)

The 16-foot deadrise *Squinx* was built by Capt. Ed Leatherbury of Shadyside, Maryland, around 1932. This shallow, V-shaped, cross-planked bottom became the style that is prominent on the bay to this day. Bay craft like this one are thought to have derived from the Hampton flattie. (Photograph by Leonard C. Rennie, courtesy of the Library of Congress.)

Sizeable dredge boats like this became the dominant boat for dredging during the heyday of the oyster harvest. A large catch required a large boat such as a schooner, bugeye, or skipjack, and a heavier boat needed more substantial steering. A wheel with a worm gear was often used. This was a simple yet stout method. With a very different feel than a tiller, it might take eight full rotations of the wheel to send the rudder hard over in either direction. (Courtesy of the Chesapeake Bay Maritime Museum.)

Oyster shell piles like this were once seen at oyster houses all over the bay. The shell was often used for chicken feed or for paving roads. Oyster shell is frequently found under the roads and sidewalks in Baltimore. The Now image shows oyster house in Crisfield operating during the peak season, in the middle of the winter. (Courtesy of the Library of Congress.)

Tongers are working off of a dory. Earlier dories had one or two masts and sails and then were converted to power. In the modern photograph, carpenters are preparing for some fine work on an old dory. (Then photograph by Arthur Rothenstein, courtesy of the Library of Congress; now photograph courtesy of the Chesapeake Bay Maritime Museum.)

This spotless bugeye has been converted for tonging. The oysters are dumped onto the culling board and sorted, keeping the adults to take to market. Hang-tonging is still done today in the shallow waters that are off-limits to dredgers. (Photograph by Leonard C. Rennie, courtesy of the Library of Congress.)

These tongers are off-loading at the pier, a scene that still goes on in the late afternoon hours all over the bay. Now one will usually see a conveyor belt and refrigerator truck. The gant line, for hauling in the basket, is often powered by an electric motor. Not much has changed. (Photograph by Leonard C. Rennie, courtesy of the Library of Congress.)

Dories are rafted up to a market boat or buy boat. The first buy boats were converted schooners turned into power vessels. Visible are the distinguishing features, which include the wheelhouse and the topping lift. Buy boats are no longer used as middlemen since the dwindling catch has rendered them obsolete. Workboats now take their catch directly to the piers, where a refrigerator truck will be waiting. (Photograph by Leonard C. Rennie, courtesy of the Library of Congress.)

This dory is off-loading at the pier. In the Now picture, the skipjack *Somerset* is off-loading in Wenonah. She is one of six skipjacks still dredging. These boats are catching about 80 bushels on a good day. (Photograph by Leonard C. Rennie, courtesy of the Library of Congress.)

The modern and more utilized method of oystering this day is patent tonging. A hydraulic tonging rig is fixed to a deadrise boat. One person can operate this rig, using his feet to open, close, and lower the tongs. The oysters are dumped onto a culling board just like they have been since the log canoe days. The picture below was taken in the early 1980s; the same method is still used. (Courtesy of the Chesapeake Bay Maritime Museum.)

Here is a good example of a box stern deadrise— the most common style today. This picture of the patent tonger was taken from a skipjack. Many patent tongers have converted their rigs with dredges. More beds have been opened to power dredging, which is believed to clean the silt off for a better spat set. (Courtesy of the Chesapeake Bay Maritime Museum.)

This oysterman is selling his catch at the McNasby Oyster Company in Eastport, Annapolis. He is placing oysters on the engine box to keep track of how many bushels were off-loaded. A bushel holds about 200 oysters. The oyster house dates back to the beginning of the 20th century and was the last one to operate in Annapolis. It is now in the Annapolis Maritime Museum. (Photograph by Robert de Gast, courtesy of the Chesapeake Bay Maritime Museum.)

CRABBING AND OTHER FISHERIES

Although oysters were once the dominant catch in the Chesapeake Bay, crabs have now moved prominently into the spotlight. In 2004, Maryland harvested over 33 million pounds of crab and only about 63,000 pounds of oyster meat. Other fish, such as clams, eels, and fin fish are also gathered by watermen. Today's deadrise workboat is used for most of these, adapting the rig to suit the job. (Courtesy of the Library of Congress.)

Wire baskets full of hard crabs are ready to be placed in a steamer before being picked. Crab houses like this would have a dock where workboats could directly sell their catch. It is still much the same with the J. M. Clayton Company in Cambridge. Founded in 1890, it is the last of 20 crab houses remaining and is one of the few working originals. (Photograph by A. Aubrey Bodine, © Jennifer Bodine, courtesy of www.AAubreyBodine.com.)

This is a drake tail, or duck tail, from Hooper Island. When these boats were being built, they were considered the fastest of their kind, having a narrow beam and long waterline. It is said that some builders used wagon wheels to create the curved rail on the stern. Wingate, Maryland, boat builder Bronza Parks, who was highly regarded for his work, built the drake tail *Martha*. (Courtesy of the Chesapeake Maritime Museum.)

These crabbers are speeding away on their drake tail. As the engines became more powerful, the sterns tended to squat, or dip down. This captain has attached a platform that extends aft on the waterline, helping to prevent squatting. (Photograph by Reginald Hotchkiss, courtesy of the Library of Congress.)

Crab scrapes are used to gather peeler crabs, or shedding crabs, in Maryland's lower bay, particularly Tangier Sound. Pulled by a small workboat, they drag over the underwater grasses where the vulnerable peelers hide. This does not damage the grasses, which are vital to the health of the bay. Crab pots are used in deeper waters to catch the hard crabs. These traps are baited to lure them in. They are marked by a small float tethered to the pot. (Photograph by A. Aubrey Bodine, © Jennifer Bodine, courtesy of www.AAubreyBodine.com.)

Over the years, watermen have been improving their boats. Traditionally steering was aft and over the rudder post. Later a stick mounted on one side of the boat was used so that the watermen could simultaneously work the fishing gear and steer. A small wheelhouse is also typically seen for protecting the driver while getting to and from the fishing grounds. (Photograph by Leonard C. Rennie, courtesy of the Library of Congress.)

This man is crabbing off his ducktail boat. The method is trot-lining and is mainly done in the protected rivers and creeks of the Chesapeake Bay. Bait is tied along the length of a line up to a quarter of a mile long, and then the line is laid along the bottom of the water. On either end of the line are weights with buoys. After soaking them, the waterman starts at one end and places the lines over a block on the boat. As he moves ahead, crabs come up clamped onto the bait. They are scooped up with a dip net made of chicken wire. These are preferred over mesh nets, for they always stay open. Trot lining is still widely used to this day. (Courtesy of Caryl Firth, Chesapeake Bay Maritime Museum.)

A typical scene shows wooden deadrise boats in a waterman's town. Now some captains choose to use the easier-maintained fiberglass workboat. Although of a different construction, they have retained the same basic style and shape. (Photograph by A. Aubrey Bodine, © Jennifer Bodine, courtesy of www.AAubreyBodine.com.)

CRABBING AND OTHER FISHERIES

In 1952, the Maryland clam dredge was put into use harvesting soft shell clams or maninose. The rig consists of a conveyer belt with a high-pressure water hose at the lower end. This contraption is attached to a deadrise boat. The forward end is lowered, and the hose digs a trench in which the belt scrapes along, scooping up clams. The same method is still used. (Photograph by A. Aubrey Bodine, © Jennifer Bodine, courtesy of www.AAubreyBodine.com.)

These men are pulling up a pound net and gathering fish. Nets, attached to wood stakes, are used to trap the fish. The traps are set from April to November in about 12 to 20 feet of water. Fiberglass boats are now often used for this purpose. (Gift of Dr. Harry Walsh, Chesapeake Bay Maritime Museum.)

CRABBING AND OTHER FISHERIES

CHAPTER 3

WORKBOAT HARBORS

Working harbors range from the quaint Oxford to the busy, industrial Baltimore. While some have changed very little through the years, many may be unrecognizable now. Several watermen towns have suffered with the decline of harvest and, more recently, have been revived with new waterfront housing and businesses. Baltimore has seen many changes throughout the years. Pictured is the Pratt Street oyster wharf, which is now Harbor Place—a popular tourist attraction and home to numerous businesses. (Courtesy of the Library of Congress.)

REPAIRING OYSTER BOATS
CRISFIELD, MD.

Oysterboats are hauled out at a Crisfield yard. Only the remnants of the old railways are usually seen these days. Most of the old yards now cater to yachts. (Courtesy of the Wittemann Collection, Library of Congress.)

This bridge spans Knapp's Narrows, which separates Tilghman Island from the Bay Hundred peninsula. Boaters will often use the narrows as a shortcut to travel in and out of the Choptank River. The first bridge was built in 1843. The one pictured in the Then photograph now spans the entrance to the Chesapeake Bay Maritime Museum. (Courtesy of the William and Otelia G. Bodenstein, Chesapeake Bay Maritime Museum.)

Here is the J. C. Lore and Sons Oyster House in Solomon's Island in 1980. Skipjacks *Ruby G. Ford* and *Martha Lewis* along with tonger *Miss Michelle* can be seen. Originally founded in 1888 by Joseph C. Lore Sr., this building dates back to 1934. It is now owned by the Calvert Marine Museum, which holds various exhibits there. (Courtesy of the Calvert Marine Museum.)

Capt. William Burke Vane and Capt. Allen P. Vane came to Baltimore from the Eastern Shore in 1898 to open a chandlery in Fell's Point. They previously owned and supplied bay craft for 40 years. In 1910, the business was moved to 602–604 Pratt Street, across from Long Dock. The area is now a popular shopping and night spot district. (Courtesy of Vane Brothers.)

The Vane Brothers Chandlery was moved from Pratt Street to 916 South Broadway—the old immigration building. This was finally a location where they could directly service vessels. Coincidently this was next door to the original chandlery. The latest facility was recently built with up-to-date, modern equipment. (Courtesy of Vane Brothers.)

Originally called Annemessex, then Somers Cove, the town of Crisfield was named for John W. Crisfield, who recognized the close proximity to many oyster beds and pushed for the Eastern Shore Railroad from Salisbury to there. This in turn made it "the seafood capital of the world." Since the decline of oysters, the town is now known as "the crab capital of the world." The cove is surrounded by packinghouses that were built on oyster shells. Now much of the waterfront is towered over by condominiums. (Courtesy of the Jack Kelbaugh collection, Chesapeake Bay Maritime Museum.)

Taken around 1940, this photograph shows a bugeye and a skipjack in Cambridge at the end of the season. The harbor was once home to many dredge boats. Only a few remain. (Photograph by A. Aubrey Bodine, © Jennifer Bodine, courtesy of www.AAubreyBodine.com.)

Originally a shallow waterway surrounded by marsh, Kent Narrows was first dredged in 1876, connecting the Chester River with Eastern Bay. Still a thriving waterman's port, it is also shared with several restaurants and condos. (Courtesy of the Chesapeake Bay Maritime Museum.)

This photograph was taken in 1909, during the heyday of oyster harvesting. The region's record catch was set the year before at 11 million bushels. This period included the peak of Oxford's boatbuilding industry. Although still a waterman's town, yachting has boomed here over the years. The prestigious Hinkley Yacht Company has a yard here. Cults and Case Shipyard is also building some fine wooden boats in the area. (Courtesy of the Jack Kelbaugh collection, Chesapeake Bay Maritime Museum.)

This 1921 photograph shows the fruit pier on Pratt Street, also called the new pier after it was rebuilt following the 1904 fire, when the old wharves were burned. It was later the site of the United Fruit Company. They shipped in bananas and pineapples from the Caribbean and South America. (Courtesy of the Jack Kelbaugh collection, Chesapeake Bay Maritime Museum.)

Fruit Pier on Pratt Street, Baltimore, Md.

Below, one can see the oyster fleet crowded around the first few piers of Pratt Street. The proximity to several saloons made this an ideal location for shanghaiing crew. Proprietors were often in cahoots with captains and would sell them an unsuspecting drunk man. During these times, many men woke up on a dredge boat only to be put to work. To the left, one can just see the steamboats at Light Street. The area was filled in about 330 feet by the 1970s. Now it is the home of Harborplace Mall and the Promenade. The modern photograph shows one of Harborplace's popular tourist attractions—Baltimore's dragonboat fleet. (Courtesy of the Charles T. Precht Sr. collection, Chesapeake Bay Maritime Museum.)

BALTIMORE. Harbor, Showing Oyster Fleet.

Grain Elevators and Piers, Canton Harbor, Baltimore, Md.

Pictured here are the grain elevator and piers of North Locust Point around 1916. A fire destroyed the building in 1922. The newer grain elevator was recently converted into high-rise condominiums. (Courtesy of the Chesapeake Bay Maritime Museum.)

The Annapolis City Dock was once a haven for workboats. In the summer one would see crabbing boats; then, come November first, the skipjacks would take over. Now called Ego Alley, workboats have been replaced with yachts. The pleasure boats are drawn to this spot for many of the same reasons: shelter and convenience. (Photograph by A. Aubrey Bodine, courtesy of www.AAubreyBodine.com.)

Here Spa Creek in Annapolis is visible in a photograph taken from around the end of First Street in Eastport. The moored boats appear to be log canoes. One can just make out the old bridge, top left, and St. Mary's Church, top right. Today in the summertime the moorings will be occupied by yachts. (Courtesy of the Chesapeake Bay Maritime Museum.)

The town of Solomon's Island was not of much significance until its namesake, Isaac Solomon, established a cannery in 1867. This coincided with the oyster boom, and the area became famous for building bugeyes. Close to what was once the M. M. Davis Shipyard is now the facility for the Cove Point liquid natural gas terminal tugboats. (Courtesy of the Calvert Marine Museum.)

CHAPTER 4

CARGO

Ever since Maryland was first settled, people have been using boats to transport goods. Before the days of highways and trucks, the practical method of hauling cargo such as coal, lumber, and produce was by boats like the ram *Edwin and Maud* (pictured). Rams were narrow, long schooners built especially to fit through the Chesapeake and Delaware Canal. (Gift of Lester Trott, Chesapeake Bay Maritime Museum.)

The bugeye *Florence* is off-loading watermelons at Port Covington in Baltimore. *Emma Giles* is in the background. The pungy schooner *Lady Maryland* is a replica of the type of boat that often carried produce. It is said that they were painted pink and green to advertise the sale of watermelons. (Photograph by A. Aubrey Bodine, © Jennifer Bodine, courtesy of www.AAubreyBodine.com.)

The schooner *Columbia* is unloading lumber at Long Dock in this photograph from 1936. Federal Hill is in the background. Much of Baltimore was built with lumber carried on schooners such as this. The load often came from North Carolina or Georgia. The boat's booms would be lifted to accommodate the cargo, and the sailors would have to stand on top to work the sails. (Photograph by Arthur A. Moorshead, courtesy of the Chesapeake Bay Maritime Museum.)

Long Dock is on Pier Four in the heart of Baltimore's Inner Harbor. Bay boats brought produce from the rural areas of the Chesapeake here. Better roads and trucks made this scene of crowded boats obsolete. Once paid, the crew often took the opportunity to patronize the saloons and brothels just a few blocks away on Baltimore Street, then to later go home penniless and hung over. Photographs of Long Dock are easily recognizable by the four sticks of the Steam Plant of East Baltimore, otherwise known as the Powerplant. It was built between 1900 and 1909 to power the trolley cars and then, about 1920, to provide steam to heat downtown buildings. Today the edifice is still the most prominent part of the Inner Harbor, but instead of power it now provides entertainment. (Courtesy of the Jack Kelbaugh collection, Chesapeake Bay Maritime Museum.)

Harbor Scene. Baltimore, Md.

Taken sometime in the late 1930s, this schooner would have most likely been used for bay or coastal trade. Today small cargo ships carry more and make dependable transits. (Photograph by Leonard C. Rennie, courtesy of the Library of Congress.)

This photograph shows the steam freighter *Louise* sailing out of the Inner Harbor, Baltimore. She was with the Ericsson Line and sailed between Philadelphia and Baltimore before World War II. Now, with improved highways and railways, freight often comes in from overseas and is then loaded on trucks and trains for further transport. (Courtesy of the Chesapeake Bay Maritime Museum.)

The bugeye *L. F. Petty* is loading cordwood at Smith Creek. Loading freight was once a slow and arduous task. Now it is much more efficient, with modular pieces of cargo on container ships. Containers are pre-packed and trucked to the terminal, where cranes quickly place them on board. Each ship has only about a 12- to 24-hour turnaround. (Photograph by John Collier, courtesy of the Library of Congress.)

This schooner-rigged vessel is the ram *Edwin and Maude*. Rams were specially built to transit through the then-narrow Chesapeake and Delaware Canal. These bulk carriers were used to transport everything from logwood to coal up and down the coast. She is now the *Victory Chimes*, sailing passengers out of Maine. Today the ram has been replaced with the very practical tug and barge. This is the barge *Portsmouth* being pushed by K-Sea's tug *North Sea*. She had just unloaded ore at Sparrow's Point, Baltimore. (Gift of Lester Trott, Chesapeake Bay Maritime Museum.)

CARGO

Early tugs and barges were simple and not user-friendly. Often the barges were the converted hulls of outdated sailing vessels. These days, they have become very sophisticated. Push boats, with square bows, and articulated tugs and barges are often used. The articulated tug and barge uses a barge with a notch on the stern. The tug fits into the notch and extends "pins" out of either side of its bow and into the barge. The result is a more rigid unit that can still pitch with the seas efficiently. (Courtesy of the Chesapeake Bay Maritime Museum.)

C. Duff Hughes is seen christening the 42,000-gallon motor tanker *Duff* in 1971. He is the son of Charles Hughes Sr. Claude and Charles Hughes Sr., cousins of the Vane brothers, became partners in the Vane Brothers Chandlery in 1920. When Duff Hughes became a junior partner, he recognized the potential for growth in the marine fuel trade and concentrated efforts there with great success. The tanker *Duff* is now being retired from the fleet after serving a long career. (Courtesy of Vane Brothers.)

In this photograph, the deck of the ram *Levin J. Marvel* is visible. The necessary rigging makes a barge all the more appealing for loading and working. (Gift of Lester Trott, Chesapeake Bay Maritime Museum.)

Below, one can see North Locust Point, which is now Tide Point and Domino Sugar. German, Irish, and later Polish immigrants sailed into Locust Point, where they could board a B&O train to points west or take the ferry directly across to Fells Point or other East Coast cities. Many immigrants were duped into working on oyster dredging boats for little to no pay. (Courtesy of the Chesapeake Bay Maritime Museum.)

CHAPTER 5

PASSENGERS

This was a common sight before the days of highways and airplanes. Bay steamers worked day and night connecting small towns and big cities, bringing passengers and cargo. The steamer *Dorchester* is seen making a stopover in St. Mary's at the Wharf Bromes. (Courtesy of the Chesapeake Bay Maritime Museum.)

Taken sometime in the early 1960s, this photograph shows the *Provincetown* (right), *General* (left front), and the *Potomac* (left back). The Powerplant can be seen in the background. Not long after this photograph was taken, a Baltimore businessman purchased *Provincetown* and renamed her *Chesapeake*, hoping to revive passenger service on the bay. The plan was to have her operating between Washington, D.C., and Lower Bay, accommodating 200 passengers while providing staterooms, food, and entertainment. The demands by the Coast Guard for repairs proved too costly, ending the venture. (Gift of Michael H. Osborne, Chesapeake Bay Maritime Museum.)

The very busy terminal on Light Street is where Harborplace Mall is today. Much like the modern airport, one could travel to all parts of the bay and connect to other cities on the East Coast and the rest of the world. In the background to the left is Federal Hill. On top of the hill, one can just make out the old signal tower. This was in sight of a tower on North Point at the mouth of the Patapsco River. When the boats were spotted coming up the bay, the North Point tower signaled with flags to Federal Hill. They in turn raised flags to signal which companies' boats were arriving—a simple system with the only problem occurring in times of poor visibility. (Courtesy of the Jack Kelbaugh collection, Chesapeake Bay Maritime Museum.)

The Broadway Ferry connected the short span to North Locust Point between about 1813 and 1939. It brought immigrants to Fells Point and took workers to the B&O Railroad and coal piers, among others. The ferry pictured appears to be the *Samual W. Tagart*, which operated between 1878 and the early 1900s. Paved roads and streetcars brought an end to that ferry service, and now the pier is used for transient yachts, tugs, and visiting ships. (Courtesy of the Chesapeake Bay Maritime Museum.)

BROADWAY FERRY.

From left to right, Pratt Street steamers *Calvert*, *Eastern Shore*, and *Piankatank* lay idle at Pier 1 after a night run up the bay in 1936. This photograph was taken during the last days of operating as bay steamers. Previously with the grand Baltimore and Virginia Steamboat Company, these boats were being operated between 1933 and 1939 by the Baltimore, Crisfield, and Onancock Line, a last-ditch effort to revive an industry being displaced by trucks and buses. Sadly, these boats all met an end, by being either converted to barges or broken up. Today's passenger boats take people out for harbor tours. (Gift of Michael H. Osborne, Chesapeake Bay Maritime Museum.)

This photograph shows the ram *Levin J. Marvel* sailing out of Annapolis. Here she has been converted to a dude cruiser, which takes out passengers, giving them a chance to work the sails. The radio towers seen in the background are a familiar landmark to sailors transiting the bay. Vessels like *Clipper City* still provide this service today. (Courtesy of the Chesapeake Bay Maritime Museum.)

In what was once a common scene around the bay, the steamboat *Mohawk* is busy unloading passengers at this unidentified wharf. Obsolete now, remnants of piers can still be seen in many once bustling towns. During those days, much of the population experienced the bay's wonders. Now it is mainly limited to recreational boaters. Today many passenger vessels are harbor-tour boats. (Courtesy of the T. Holmes collection, Chesapeake Bay Maritime Museum.)

In 1912, the first bay ferry to connect Annapolis and Claiborne was the 105-foot steam yacht *Texas*, built in 1889. By 1942, the landing was moved from Annapolis to Sandy Point, shaving off 25 minutes. At this time, the previously problematic service was finally running efficiently when the Bay Bridge was proposed and built. On July 31, 1952, while Gov. Theodore R. McKeldin led the dedication drive, the ferry *Harry W. Nice* (pictured) made her last run between Sandy Point and Matapeake, Kent Island. She is now in Seattle, Washington, as the *Olympic*. The Sandy Point Pier is still intact and is used by the bridge construction equipment. (Courtesy of the Chesapeake Bay Maritime Museum.)

Started in 1683, the Oxford Bellevue Ferry shuttles passengers across the Tred Avon River to 7 miles outside of St. Michael's. Earlier ferries were often dugout canoes. Later two canoes were lashed together in order to take wagons across. Pictured from 1989 is a crude yet effective way to convert a ferry into a fireboat. Today the same ferry, *Talbot*, is still as busy as ever, making about 25 trips a day and carrying up to nine cars at a time. Cyclists also benefit from the ferry. (Courtesy of the William G. Bodenstein collection, Chesapeake Bay Maritime Museum.)

This small ferry on the Wicomico River (above) uses a cable attached to either shore and laid on the bottom to guide it back and forth. An engine pulls it along its cable. Ferries like this are still being used in rural areas today—like the one below on the Nanticoke River. (Courtesy of the Chesapeake Bay Maritime Museum.)

CHAPTER 6

BOATYARDS

Workboat yards at one time were plentiful on the Chesapeake Bay. Most have been abandoned or converted to yacht yards. Pictured is the old Crisfield Railway. Remnants of old railways can often be seen, usually abandoned for the more efficient travel lift. (Courtesy of the Chesapeake Bay Maritime Museum.)

These men are roughly shaping the butt end of a mast at the Jim Richardson boatyard. Now modern power equipment is being used at the Chesapeake Maritime Museum, saving much in labor and time. (Then photograph by Robert de Gast; both courtesy of the Chesapeake Bay Maritime Museum.)

The traditional method of stepping the mast on a skipjack is to place the boat between two other skipjacks. The halyards are tied to the mast, then raised and lowered into place. In the event there are no other skipjacks handy, a crane is used. (Courtesy of the Chesapeake Bay Maritime Museum.)

Caulking or "corking" is an old tradition still used today on wooden boats. Often these cross-planked, flat-bottom boats were not caulked in the plank seams, but instead the planks were installed with a snug fit and later swelled tight after being in the water for a while. Caulking mallets and irons are used to pound the cotton and oakum into the seam for a watertight seal. (Photograph by Robert de Gast, courtesy of Chesapeake Bay Maritime Museum.)

These skipjacks are hauled out on traditional railways. Timbers are lowered down to make rails that lead at an angle into the water. The boat is run on top of these timbers, which are pulled along with the boat out of the water by a motorized winch. The photograph below is at Hartge Yacht Yard, which is still a working and very busy yard. (Above photograph by Robert de Gast, courtesy of Chesapeake Bay Maritime Museum.)

The Smith Shipyard, located on Curtis Bay, has been operating for over 100 years. During the last days of sail, they specialized in converting schooners into power vessels. One could identify their conversions by the unique "Smith wheelhouse." In this photograph, the hauled-out motor tanker *Vane Brothers* is visible. The shipyard offers a variety of services, which include the supplying of marine barges and cranes. They are also capable of repairing barges up to 375 feet and tugs up to 120 feet. (Courtesy of Vane Brothers.)

Workboats are often repaired and painted before the start of a new season. The boats are then put "overboard," which simply means slid back into the water. The sailing workboats will usually participate in a race, a good way to test the equipment before the working season. (Photograph by Robert de Gast, courtesy of the Chesapeake Bay Maritime Museum.)

At the old J. O. Lore yard in Solomon's Island, J. O. Lore is on the right, Linwood Langley is seated, and Capt. Leon Langley is at the top of the hill. It is now Zahniser's Yachting Center. The old railway has been bulkheaded and replaced with a travel lift. The old building can still be seen. (Courtesy of the Calvert Marine Museum.)

WHERE ARE THEY NOW?

Thousands of bay boats have come and gone, never to be remembered. Some have fallen into disrepair to the point of no return, while others may never have been regarded as more than just objects to work, only to be later disposed of when they were no longer productive. The boats being preserved today are being maintained in different ways. Whether privately, through a nonprofit, or by a museum, it is more important that they are being cared for, thus retaining part of our culture. Pictured here is the three-sail bateau *Mamie Mister*. (Courtesy of the Chesapeake Bay Maritime Museum.)

Kathryn was built in 1901 at Crisfield, Maryland. Unlike most skipjacks, she has a rounded chine. For many years, her home port was Knapps Narrows in Tilghman Island. She was recently sold and now resides in Deal Island. The new owners intend to dredge her again. (Photograph by Jim Lowe, courtesy of the Library of Congress.)

One of the most reputable boat builders on the Bay, Bronza Parks, built three skipjacks side by side—*Rosie Parks*, *Martha Lewis*, and *Lady Katie*—also known as the three sisters. Pictured is *Rosie Parks*, completed in 1954 for Capt. Orville Parks. She was a huge success both at working and at racing. It was said that she had won the workboat races so many years in a row that the other captains started to conspire against Captain Parks in order to share the glory. *Rosie* was later donated to the Chesapeake Bay Maritime Museum, which is making plans for her restoration. (Courtesy of the Chesapeake Bay Maritime Museum.)

Distinguished by dredge
boat license No. 1, the
Hilda M.Willing was
built in 1905 at Oriole,
Maryland. Pete Sweitzer
was also known for having
the sail-dredge-only law
changed to be able to
power dredge twice a
week, thus saving many
skipjacks from extinction.
Hilda is still owned
and dredged today by
Sweitzer's son. (Courtesy
of the Chesapeake Bay
Maritime Museum.)

WHERE ARE THEY NOW?

This is a Pot Pie skiff built by George Jackson of Wittman, Maryland. She was built for Lock Brando, who used her for about 30 years. Skiffs are utility boats that are often used for crabbing or oystering in small quantities. The Pot Pie is a good example of a tuck stern, where the bottom corners are "tucked" in. She is now part of the Chesapeake Bay Maritime Museum's waterman's dock display. (Courtesy of the Chesapeake Bay Maritime Museum.)

The *William B. Tennison* was first built as a bugeye in 1899 on Crab Island by Frank Laird. She was soon sold and in 1902 moved to Virginia, where she was turned into a buy boat just five years later. In 1920, while hauling sweet potatoes from the Carolinas, *Tennison* collided with a tug on the Albemarle Sound, sustaining damage to her port side. The tug captain was said to have been drunk. The Lore packing company bought her in 1945, bringing the boat back to Maryland. Now the Calvert Marine Museum takes care of her while taking passengers out on tours. (Photograph by A. Aubrey Bodine, © Jennifer Bodine, courtesy of www.AAubreyBodine.com.)

WHERE ARE THEY NOW?

Built just over the state line in Virginia, the *H. M. Krentz* was based on the lines of the *Fannie L. Daughtery*. The boat was built by her namesake at the Krentz boatyard. This was the only skipjack that he built, but he repaired many. When put side by side with a skipjack from the upper bay, one can see that the *Krentz* has a higher bow. Also known as a Virginia bow, it was made for the rougher waters around the Potomac. Today she does a combination of dredging and carrying passengers. (Courtesy of the Chesapeake Bay Maritime Museum.)

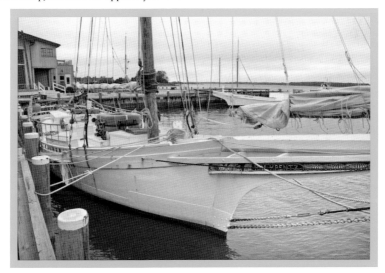

The buy boat *Mildred Belle* was built in 1948 and named for the first owner's daughters, Mildred Lee and Hattie Belle Evans. Before she was built, yellow pine logs were dragged to a salt marsh, where they soaked for a year. They were then dried out and used for planks in her construction. In 1988, she was purchased from the Chesapeake Bay Maritime Museum by Living Classrooms Foundation, which currently uses her as a floating classroom. (Courtesy of the Chesapeake Bay Maritime Museum.)

The four-masted schooner *Doris Hamlin* was built in 1919 and bought by Capt. William Burke Vane in 1931. Because of the Depression, she did not get any work until the following summer. Her first voyage was an expedition to the Caribbean with several undergrad students. It was headed by L. Ron Hubbard, who later founded Scientology. When World War II hit, she got more work but was later believed to be sunk by a German U-boat.

The new *Doris Hamlin* is a push boat built in 1980. She is 88 feet long and has a beam of 38 feet, which just happens to be the same width as her namesake. Vane Brothers acquired her in 1998 and works her today. (Then photograph by A. Aubrey Bodine, © Jennifer Bodine, courtesy of www.AAubreyBodine.com; Now courtesy of Vane Brothers.)

Martha Lewis is loaded down with oysters. Built in 1955 by Bronza Parks, she has never missed a dredge season except during her 1994 restoration. She still sail-dredges to this day, while other skipjacks use their push boats. It is believed that *Martha Lewis* is the last working sailboat to work under sail in North America. (Photograph by Robert de Gast, courtesy of the Chesapeake Bay Maritime Museum.)

The skipjack *Stanley Norman* is seen here lying at the Annapolis City Dock. The boat was built in 1902 in Salisbury, Maryland, by Otis Lloyd and named for his two sons, Stanley and Norman. She was owned and dredged for a while by Capt. Ed Farley before being sold to her current owner, the Chesapeake Bay Foundation. She still operates from the city dock and is used for education programs. (Courtesy of the Chesapeake Bay Maritime Museum.)

The last of the three sisters to be completed was *Lady Katie* in 1956. The man who commissioned her died before her completion. Bronza decided to keep *Lady Katie*, working her and taking his family for outings. She is now at the Chesapeake Bay Maritime Museum, nearing complete restoration for current owner Scott Todd. (Courtesy of the Chesapeake Bay Maritime Museum.)

The ram *Edward R. Baird Jr.* is pictured at the end of her career in Tangier Sound in 1955. While many boats have been taken by the elements, never to be brought back, several are being preserved. In our fast-paced modern culture, several traditions have fallen by the wayside. The bay area still has a thriving interest in its culture. This can be seen at skipjack and log canoe races, museums, and boatbuilding programs, to name just a few. There is a great hope for the future of bay craft. (Photograph by Leonard C. Rennie, courtesy of the Library of Congress.)

DISCOVER THOUSANDS OF LOCAL HISTORY BOOKS
FEATURING MILLIONS OF VINTAGE IMAGES

Arcadia Publishing, the leading local history publisher in the United States, is committed to making history accessible and meaningful through publishing books that celebrate and preserve the heritage of America's people and places.

Find more books like this at
www.arcadiapublishing.com

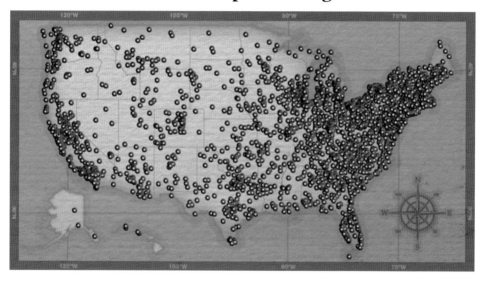

Search for your hometown history, your old stomping grounds, and even your favorite sports team.

Consistent with our mission to preserve history on a local level, this book was printed in South Carolina on American-made paper and manufactured entirely in the United States. Products carrying the accredited Forest Stewardship Council (FSC) label are printed on 100 percent FSC-certified paper.

MADE IN THE USA